Table of Contents

All the different teas such as black tea, green tea, pu'erh tea and white tea come from the same evergreen tree, *Camellia sinensis*. Each of these teas is processed differently to achieve the different types. Locations where they are grown and when they are harvested also play a role in their quality and taste.

Tea is arguably the most popular beverage in the world. It has shaped entire cultures and even fueled wars. Harvesting, processing and even making tea has evolved for thousands of years and is considered a high art form.

In the tea industry, tea makers blend various ingredients (to include teas) to create unique teas that we come to love and enjoy. Artisan blenders take things a step further and create tea blends that are proprietary to a tea brand or tea shop or for individuals.

Some online tea retailers even provide the option for their customers to create a blend based on several choices of teas, herbs, and infusions. You can get as wild and funky as you want by creating tea blends. However, the flavor is the end goal in any blend creation.

For major tea companies, it is paramount that each batch of its English Breakfast taste the same as the previous one, so that when a consumer next purchase the same tea he/she will not be able to detect a difference in flavour. Tea is also a very fragile plant with the ability to easily receive any aroma, which works against it sometimes during the manufacturing process or transportation. Tea blenders will however be able to use this fragility to our advantage and stabilize it to create beautiful blends. Tea blending is a fun craft that any tea drinker can learn with a simple guide.

About 90% of the tea varieties that are sold in the UK happen to be brands that are prepared by concocting or blending up to a maximum of 30-35 distinct varieties. These brands are highly sought after by those who struggle to start their day without first having their morning cuppa, and are easily available in most shops and supermarkets. The blended brands are popular because of their consistency with respect to flavor, character, and quality.

Each and every blended tea brand is prepared using a recipe that is unique and exclusive. Companies that own and market their brands are fiercely protective about the recipes and would go to any length to keep the formula a trade secret. The tea blender who has extensive experience of tasting teas is responsible for ensuring the blend(s) of his or her firm satisfies all quality parameters.

Tea blending is an essential aspect and part of the tea industry. It is what makes tea commercial and appealing to a larger number of consumers. Tea blending is also considered to be art, with a principle of creating the perfect taste, appearance and aroma for each and every buyer and tea consumer.

The principle itself is based on the inspection of the possible and desired taste and aroma, the actual tea combination and the consistent production of the same tea blend for years to come. However, without the proper tea selection, weighing and arrangement, tea blending principles don't mean a lot. To create a specific tea blend or combination takes a lot of hard work, knowledge, and experience in all sorts of tea. One needs to understand the variety of tea, the grade, origin, quality, processing of the tea, and its possible interaction with other teams and herbs.

As tea blending is extremely interesting, and also possible for you to do at home, we are going to take a look at this topic in detail. We're going to explore the blending techniques, how you can blend and scent tea at home as well as what tea blending process consists of. Hopefully, we'll inspire you to try some new tea blends or to start blending tea at home. So, without further ado, let's get started.

CHAPTER ONE

The Basics of Blending

Every blend uses one ingredient as a base. This is usually a pure real teas or dried herbs that connect all flavors together. Fresh flavors of mint, spearmint, lemongrass and tangy and sour lemon, hibiscus and strawberries are great for summer teas, while spices make perfect warming winter teas. Black and rooibos teas blend well with sweet ingredients, and green tea with sour, fruity and fresh ingredients.

What Is Tea Blending?

By definition, tea blending is the simple process of putting teas of different characteristics together to form a final product. The golden rule of tea blending is to achieve consistency in taste, while reflecting nuances of it's different components.

Classically, tea blending is associated with black tea production. As tea companies require a specific taste for their house black tea [English Breakfast], Tea Tasters in Sri Lanka & India would have to create and maintain unique black tea blends for the tea companies, also known as a "Standard" in the industry.

Brief History of Tea Blending

Tea blends came about for two reasons; first to introduce new and unique tastes, aromas, and textures to a cup of tea. This is the fun, creative, and/or medicinal aspect of tea blending.

Secondly, tea blends make it possible to have absolute consistency in a pot of tea; from cup to cup, year to year, decade to decade. Since tea is an agricultural crop it can vary from year to year. It is only through blending various ingredients to balance the blend that this consistency can be achieved.

Purists may turn up their noses at tea blends; but the enjoyment of tea blends is almost as old as the discovery of tea itself. The Chinese have been making tea blends for 2500 years. The first book on tea, The Classic of Tea, by Lu Yu published around 760 A.D. talks of many items (mostly herbs and medicinals) that can be blended with tea. Two of the most famous tea blends are Jasmine tea and Earl Grey tea, both going back hundreds of years.

Traditionally, a given geographic area would blend into their tea whatever was produced or available locally. Southeastern China would blend in orange peels from their citrus groves. Tibet would blend in yak butter and salt. Indians would blend in local spices like cardamom, pepper, ginger. Eastern Europeans would blend in local fruits and berries.

Tea Blending Techniques

Blending is not a modern innovation; mixing tea with herbs and spices has been around for hundreds of years. Nonetheless, tea blending has become increasingly popular in the recent decade, as the modern tea consumer always searches for new and interesting tea blends, with unique taste and aroma. That is why tea blending techniques evolve constantly; there are numerous, innovating ways tea sellers blend and combine tea.

However, to learn about tea blending means knowing what the basic tea blending techniques are. Three main blending techniques include;

Blending Herbs

The most common blending technique includes the blending of different types of herbs. The usually blended herbs are chamomile, peppermint, mint, rose, ginger, hibiscus, etc. All of the herbs (and spices) are mixed in different amounts with different tea varieties in order to create new and unique flavors. These herbal blends can also include ingredients like different plant roots, spices like cinnamon or turmeric, dried fruits, and of course, numerous varieties of herbs.

They can be blended for the purpose of unique flavors and aroma, or for the medicinal purpose. Sometimes, the tea itself is left out, so the blend only contains herbs and spices. The reason for that might lie in wanting to create decaffeinated tea, and of course, to create a purely herbal tea.

When it comes to the blending process itself, it can be done by hand, as smaller, local tea sellers do, or it can be e done in mixing drums for commercial purposes. To ensure consistency of the blend, the weight and the percentage of each ingredient in the blend is carefully observed and recorded. This way each new batch of the bland will have the same quality and identical taste, which is important if you want to keep the customers loyal to your brand.

Now, this blending technique is purely aesthetic or carries a health element. Inclusions are ingredients that add to a blend an aesthetic value as well as healthy, beneficial properties. These, however, do not alter or affect that flavor and the aroma of the blend; they just affect the chemical composition and the health properties of the blend. With inclusions, taste and aroma are actually secondary factors.

Nevertheless, if inclusions are not handled properly, or added to a blend in the right amounts, they can surely make or break your tea. Even though they do not add to the flavor and the aroma at all, they still play an important role in the blend. Tea makers are required to have exceptional blending skills to be actually allowed to be innovative with inclusions. Inclusions may not add to the flavor profile, but they surely change the color of your tea, as well as its visual appeal to you.

Tea scenting is a rather popular way of tea adopting distinct aromas from the environment where it is grown, processed and dried. Usually, tea adopts the aroma from the surrounding where they grow (like Japanese tea which grows near the sea and adapts an oceanic and vegetal flavor that becomes very distinct during the infusion); however, blending an even better way of controlling the aroma and the scent of the tea.

Scenting makes It easier to control the aroma and to add the scents based on the aroma you wish to impart. The common scents tea makers rely on are bergamot oil (usually for black tea), and jasmine 'for white and green tea). Aromatic ingredients like rose petals or lavender flowers can also be added during the drying and blending stage, and are usually left in the final blend as well.

Tea scenting

Scenting via jasmine flower is an ancient method, dating back to ancient China. Tea makers would usually use dried jasmine flowers to ensure the best-quality aroma, but sometimes even fresh flowers are used.

On the other hand, using essential oils, like bergamot, is a newer method of scenting. The oil is sprayed onto batches of leaves during the blending stage to ensure even coating and distribution. Types of essential oil used for scenting include;

- Natural essential oils (manufactured from a natural ingredient),
- Nature-identical essential oils (the same molecular make-up as natural essential oils, but made in the laboratory),
- Synthetic (made in a laboratory without matching the molecular make-up of natural essential oils).

Blending Tea at Home

Sure, it is rather easy and convenient to buy tea blends at a local store or tea shop. However, as of recently, people have started blending tea at home. Many prefer to create their own blends because it is easy to adjust the specific taste preferences, and sometimes it can be actually cheaper to create your own blend than to buy such teas. People usually choose to blend tea with herbs and spices they already have at home, which makes this process even easier. Here's how you can do it;

- Buying the ingredients – make sure to buy the herbs and spices in herbs/spice shops or in the herbs/spice aisle in the supermarket. If you're looking for more unique and specific ingredients, you can surely find them in the health food stores or on the Internet. When ordering the ingredient on the Internet, make sure that the supplier is an established, reliable supplier, who provides natural and organic ingredients.

- Using the herbs/spices you already have – if you're new to tea blending, maybe you should start with the herbs/spices you already have at home. Ingredients like peppercorns, cinnamon, cloves, ginger, chili or cacao are probably the ones you're already using in cooking. By using these ingredients, you'll get to practice creating blends, see what flavors and aromas you like, and of course, learn how to blend tea.

- Using the ingredients from your garden (or garden center) – the great thing about tea blending is that you can find the ingredients in your own garden, or purchase them at the local garden center. You can easily pluck herbs like rose petals or mint and create the so-called wet blends, using other herbs, tea, spices, roots or seeds. If you want to create a dry blend, you will simply have to let the ingredients dry by spreading them on a large tray and expose them to a warm, well-ventilated space.

- Scenting at home – if you want to scent your tea while creating a blend you can use apples, citrus peel or oil, vanilla beans, chili, star anise, turmeric, flower petals, etc. The only thing to do is to mix your tea with the scenting ingredients and leave them in an airtight container for 48 hours. If you're using the fresh scenting ingredients, make sure to remove them after you've reached the desired scent and aroma, as they will decay in the container. You can place the scenting ingredient is small muslin or paper sacs or pouches, for easier removal.

Tea Blending Tools

To begin blending tea at home, you need a few tools.

- scale

- tea spoon

- tea and other components/ingredients

- small mixing bowl

- 2-3 equal size cups, white interior (more than 1 is needed as you'll be doing side-by-side tastings)

- tea infuser/filters

- timer

- notebook and writing utensil

How is Tea Flavoured?

Tea leaves can be flavoured in many ways in making of the making of a blend.

In this introductory guide, we will be sharing with you the different methods and techniques behind the art of blending teas:

Inclusions: the direct addition of fruits, blossoms, herbs or other additives to tea leaves for the visual and/or sensory effect.

Extracts: are flavoring agents derived by extracting the essential oils from the leaves, fruits, blossoms, roots or other parts of a plant. Extracts carry the distinctive scents or flavors that we come to expect from that plant.

Natural Identical (NIs): flavoring agents that are obtained with the aid of chemical synthesis by a chemist. NIs tend to be more stable than extracts and are usually significantly less expensive. Many flavored products are flavored with nature-identical flavors.

Artificial Flavors are created by altering the chemical structure of a naturally occurring molecule to create a different & more intense compound. ETTE TEA does not use artificial flavoring agent in any of our blends.

Scenting derive their flavor simply from physical proximity to strong flavors. While some jasmine teas may be artificially flavored, "real" jasmine teas are scented with Jasmine blossoms which are then removed (jasmine blossoms have a much shorter shelf life than tea). Lapsang Souchong is scented by being exposed to the smoke of burning pine root.

Very often, these method are Combined to create our flavoured tea blends as most inclusions alter the flavor of the cup but are usually not strong enough to deliver the punch we want. Hence most "flavored" teas, are further combined with NIs. The total amount of flavouring applied depends on the flavor and desired strength, but usually falls between 0.5% - 5% of the weight of the tea being flavored.

The flavouring agent is poured or sprayed over the dry leaf subsequently mixed to ensure an even distribution. Larger companies do this in large rotating drums filled with hundreds of kilograms of tea. Most teas can be flavored (properly absorbing the extract) in under 30 minutes, though some flavors do require significantly longer.

Principles in Tea Blending

The following will be the 3 key ingredients in creating a beautiful tea blend:

- Objectives
- Balance
- Emotions

Objectives - What are we making the tea blend for? Would we want to create a wellness cocktail for the health benefits of the additives we use or simply for the gourmet & artisanal factor of creating an exquisitely crafted tea blend that brews well in a cup?

Secondly, from a technical standpoint, tea blending is about balance.

- Aesthetically beautiful dried leaves
- Rounded & balance bouquet or aroma [more applicable with extracts & NIs
- Taste & structure of the mouth-feel
- Finish

Last but not least, the most important factor in creating a tea blend is the intrinsic factor of emotions. Tea blending can be an exercise of empathy where tea leaves & herbs, when put together, are used to invoke a feeling or to tell a story of my own.

Steps to Blending Your Own Tea

Blending your own tea is a craft and takes time to prepare and carefully claim flavors in teas, spices, fruits, herbs, and flavors before you get all "mad scientist" in your kitchen. We recommend that you invest the time to become acquainted and comfortable in each step before proceeding to the next.

Popular tea blends are the result of many hours of tasting, blending, re-blending, and trying again. "Trial and error" will become your best friend.

We HIGHLY recommend that you indulge your palate with a tea journey to experience and explore various teas before embarking on tea blending. Unless you know what a certain true tea tastes like, it's impossible to effectively pair it with other ingredients.

The ingredients that go into a tea blend must be something you are familiar with in taste, sight, and pairings. Some teas or herbs may not pair well with a fruit or another tea. To help give you an idea of ideal pairings when it comes to tea, herbs, spices, and infusions (flavorings, fruit, etc.,) we have outlined a few below.

Tea Base: This will be the foundation of your tea blend that sets the tone on what type of pairings you will add. Everything should complement one another in flavor. Tea blends are very personal, and what one person likes, another may not.

Tea Base = true teas (black, green, oolong, yellow, or white)

Infusions: Infusions are elements that are added to a tea base to flavor it, enhance it, and marry it to any added herbs.

Infusions = dried/fresh fruit/fruit peel, essential oil, artificial flavoring, cacao nibs, chocolate.

Herbs: Herbs are something that requires a bit of exploring because there are various dimensions of flavors in an herb. When tasting one, ask yourself if that particular herb complements the overall tea or fights against it. Dried herbs for tea blends may taste one way out of the jar and yet another once the tea is brewed. It's best to taste the herb in both forms (dried and brewed.)

When it comes to herbs, less is more. Adding too much causes a tea to have a very unpleasant flavor (for example: too much lavender causes a soapy tasting tea.)

Herbs = dried/fresh herbs (leaves, whole plant, plant parts, flowers)

Use Caution with Herbs: Before adding herbs to your tea blends, we recommend that you do your homework on herbs and potential side effects, adverse reactions, and toxicity. This is especially important if you have any medical conditions, are taking medications, are undergoing chemotherapy, or are pregnant or nursing.

So, how do you make an herbal blend that isn't harmful? Unfortunately, we don't have the medical expertise to advise or make recommendations on what herbs to use. This is why we encourage doing a bit of research on herbs before using them.

There are hundreds of herbs that are documented as having potential harmful side effects/adverse reactions. A published research study (Dietary supplements and herbal medicine toxicities—when to anticipate them and how to manage them – Chart 2) includes a chart that lists a few herbs.

Spices: Spices are akin to "the frosting on the cake" by giving tea additional layers of flavor. Just as herbs, become well acquainted with how each tastes before adding to a tea.

Spices = dried/fresh

Have you noticed that come fall and wintertime, we tend to gravitate more towards teas that are spicy, nutty, and warming? Our preferences in teas change with seasons and our moods. When tired or depressed, a minty tea is a great pick-me-up. Summer and springtime, we are more prone to indulge in fruity, floral teas.

Fruity Blends

Season: spring, summer

Mood: happy, optimistic

Flavor profile: citrus, berry, melon, apple, pear, sweet, floral

- Tea base: Assam, Ceylon, Darjeeling, White, Yellow
- Infusion: dried/fresh strawberry, apple, peach, pear, pineapple, orange, lemon, peel, bergamot
- Herbs: chamomile, lemon verbena, mint, cornflowers, lemongrass
- Spice: sumac

Floral Blends

Season: spring, summer

Mood: melancholy, romantic, content

Flavor profile: floral, sweet, citrus

- Tea base: Oolong, White
- Infusion: dried/fresh peach, pear
- Herbs: jasmine, hibiscus, rose petals, rosehip, cornflowers, elderflower lavender (note: lavender is very strong and does best on its own without anything else added.)

Nutty Blends

Season: fall, winter

Mood: craving, nesting, solitary

Flavor profile: nutty

- Tea base: Genmaicha, Dragonwell, Rooibos
- Spice: nutmeg

Spicy Blends

Season: fall, winter

Mood: feisty, craving, festive

Flavor profile: hot, warm

- Tea base: Ceylon, Rooibos
- Spice: ginger, cloves, anise, cardamom, pepper, nutmeg, cinnamon stick

Sweet Blends

Season: spring, summer

Mood: social, energetic, bright

Flavor profile: malty, honey, melon, fruity, floral

- Tea base: Assam, White, Sencha, Oolong, Rooibos
- Herbs: chrysanthemum, rosehip, mint, honeybush
- Spice: honey

Fire Blends

Season: fall, winter

Mood: nesting, solitary, quiet

Flavor profile: cocoa, smoky, toasty, ashy

- Tea base: Hojicha, Lapsang Souchong, Ceylon, Raw Pu-erh, Rooibos
- Herbs: cacao nibs
- Spice: chocolate chips, paprika

Step #3: Gather Appropriate Equipment For Blending

There are a few things you'll need for tea blending—most of which you may already have in your kitchen.

- Shot glass (for measuring)
- Measuring spoons
- Dried spices, fruits, herbs (unless you have access to fresh)

- Note: you can dehydrate your own using a dehydrator.
- Airtight containers
- Base teas: loose-leaf true tea (such as Assam, Ceylon, Rooibos, etc.)
- Flavoring

Step #4: Begin Your Blending

NOW it's time to become that mad scientist we mentioned earlier. You can start with three of your favorite herbs. Experiment with combinations of true tea, herbs, fruits, spices, and flavorings and create something you can call your own. If you would rather play it safe and save time, there are a ton of tea blending recipes online.

Step #5: Store Your Blend Properly

It's important to store your newly blended tea in an airtight container while being careful not to include any moist/wet/damp particles or items in with the tea.

Sometimes if fresh herbs or fruits are used in a blend, it can cause the tea to become damp, which leads to mold.

Adding fresh herbs directly to your hot tea creates a bright flavor finish.

How to Create Your Own Herbal Tea Blends

There are lots of ways to enjoy the goodness of plants, but for accessibility and simplicity, it's hard to beat a good cup of tea. Herbal tea blends are a fantastic way to combine the synergistic qualities of different plant allies, and creating your own allows you to craft steepable combinations that cater to your personal nutrition goals and flavor preferences. With such a wide world of botanicals to choose from, however, it can sometimes be hard to know where to start. Luckily, we've been crafting organic tea blends for decades, and we're all too happy to share some of the strategies we've pick up along the way!

Here, we begin with a basic three step method for crafting delicious and nutritive herbal brews. Once you are comfortable with a few simple blends, it becomes easier to branch out into more complex combinations. While technically these caffeine-free herbal infusions are referred to as "tisanes" (only brews made from traditional tea leaves of the Camellia sinensis plant are true teas), we will use the term "tea" here to discuss our steeped herbal beverages.

This fun tool will help inspire and guide your adventures in creating your own tea blends from a wide range of different herbs and spices. Start by considering the motivation for creating your herbal blend; are you looking to support your immune system, encourage a relaxed state of mind, or just want to experiment with new flavors? Use your preferred herb as the "base ingredient." Then, add a "supporting" ingredient for a complementary effect or flavor. The final ingredient is an "accent" which adds a pop of flavor and can round out the other two ingredients.

These proportions are conceptual and not set in stone, so you have freedom to experiment. Start with 3 parts base ingredient, 1 to 2 parts supporting, and 1/4 to 1 part accent, and then make adjustments as needed. You will find that herbs often switch roles from one blend to the next. Feel free to begin adding additional ingredients once you are comfortable with your blending skills!

Additional research may be necessary if you are addressing specific health concerns, and we always recommend consulting a qualified medical practitioner if you are unsure of what herbs may be best for your individual needs.

Pro tips:

- Start with brewing a cup or two to test your herbal blend before mixing a larger quantity.
- Herbalism books can be wonderful starting points to help you discover blending inspiration.
- Organize a tea blending party for you and your friends to try new mixtures!

8 Homemade Tea Blends

1. Homemade Ginger Tea – Andrea at our sister site Vibrant Wellness Journal walks you through how to brew ginger tea from real ginger. She also gets into the health benefits of sipping on delicious ginger tea.

2. Homemade Herbal Tea Blends – Andrea is such a tea maven! She shared a few of her favorite homemade herbal tea recipes over at Green Living Ideas. The lemon-vanilla blend intrigues me the most!

3. Homemade Chai – Chai tea is still cool, right? I hope so, because this spiced tea blend is my favorite non-coffee hot drink. This is the hand-mixed chai recipe that I created for holiday giving a few years ago.

4. Sweet Tea Vodka – You can use hand-mixed or store-bought tea to make this robust vodka infusion. It makes a great gift for the cocktail enthusiast on your list!

5. Homemade Red Chai – Chai is a versatile tea. Seriously, this list could be just made up of different takes on this one type of homemade tea. Andrea's red chai recipe is naturally caffeine-free.

6. Mint Tea – Is the mint in your garden getting out of control? Follow these instructions to dry it, then crumble it into airtight jars to make homemade mint tea. If you need more ideas on how to use all of that garden mint, Julie's got you covered!

7. Lavender Tea – Lavender tea is fragrant and soothing, and you can make your own from the lavender in your garden! Those same drying instructions from #6 will work here.

8. Grow a Tea Garden – The last couple of teas are good examples of herbal tea ingredients that you can grow. Patricia at Eat Drink Better shares her favorite tea herbs to grow. You can turn this into a gift for gardening-inclined friends by gathering seed packets for some tea herbs and including growing instructions and brewing directions.

Mixing Up Your Tea: Which Tea Flavors Blend Best Together?

Tea is a fascinating subject. It's a plant with a range of useful health benefits, which leads many people to believe it's going to taste grassy or bland, but that couldn't be further from the truth. Sure, a plain green tea is going to taste like a plant in water, because that's all it is. The secret, though, is that you can mix up a huge array of different kinds of teas to replicate any of a million different flavors and flavor profiles.

In order to demonstrate, we've broken down tea into its core components. At the center of any tea blend is going to be your core tea. There are two types of tea: true tea and non-true tea. True tea is tea made from the tea plant, Camellia Sinensis. Other teas are actually infusions of non-tea plants, but we still call them teas because they're prepared the same way; a plant-infused beverage. Here are the different kinds of tea bases you might encounter.

True Teas:

- **White Tea:** This tea is the least processed variety of tea. Tea leaves are plucked and dried in the sunlight, then packaged and sold. It's very simple, it's typically sweet, and it's quite delicate. Sometimes it will taste almost fruity on its own, though no fruit ingredients are added.

- **Green Tea:** This is the same plant, but is processed a little more. Tea leaves are harvested, and then they're withered to dry them somewhat. After that, they are fired in a pan or in steam to further dry them. Sencha, Matcha, and Genmaicha are all varieties of green tea. This tea is typically a bit more roasted in flavor, nuttier, and greener tasting and in color.

- **Oolong Tea:** Also known as wulong tea, this is even more processed than green tea. In addition to drying, it is rolled and bruised, to release plant enzymes for oxidation. Oolong teas are often named after the regions where they are processed. They tend to taste floral and occasionally malty.

- **Black Tea:** Black teas are the most processed of the true teas, which are further rolled, bruised oxidized, and dried for processing. This results in a dark tea that tends to be more malty in flavor, and tends to include a higher caffeine content. These are also known as red teas in China.

Non-true Teas:

- **Assam:** Assam is a variety of black tea, making it technically a true tea, though purists might dispute this. It's stronger and earthier than normal black tea. Assam teas are primarily made in India rather than China.

- **Darjeeling:** Another Indian tea variant, much like Assam, this black tea is processed quickly to avoid fermentation.

- **Ceylon:** Ceylon is yet another variation on black tea, and while it's not a variation on the core plant, it is produced differently. They are primarily cultivated in Sri Lanka.

- **Purple Tea:** A very new tea that has been hitting the markets in the last few years, purple tea is a variation on black tea that is produced exclusively in Kenya at the moment. It's another variant plant, and it has a unique flavor profile tea lovers may find hooks them immediately.

- **Puer:** Also known as pu-erh tea, this is an Asian tea variety that cooks green tea immediately without drying it first, preventing oxidation. It's then aged anywhere from 10 to 50 years, which makes them ferment and then further aged.

- **Rooibos:** This is a tea made from an entirely different plant, the Aspalathus linearis plant. It's grown in South Africa and is processed in much the way black tea is produced. They are caffeine free teas and often used in chai.

- **Herbal:** Herbal teas are a huge variety of infusions that do not actually include the core tea plant. Herbal teas can contain a huge array of different plants, spices, and even fruits.

Green Tea Blends

Green blends tend to be lighter in flavor than their black cousins, but that doesn't mean they can't be bold. Greens are often fruity, but can be herbal as well.

Blend #1: Mix up some green tea with lemon peel and some freeze-dried raspberry bits for a punchy, citrusy flavor in your green tea. Raspberry stands out as a superfood as well, making this a great healthy tea option.

Blend #2: Take a green tea base and add in a handful of spices. Mix up some cinnamon with some cloves, then add in dried apple bits and orange peel. The citrus and the spice add to the basic tea base to make something resembling a candied apple in flavor.

Blend #3: Want something with citrus overtones but a smoother base? Take a green tea and blend it with apple, raspberry, and some sweet rhubarb. Then top the whole thing off with a bit of vanilla to give it that smooth finish.

Blend #4: Mix up a base of green sencha and rooibos teas, then add in some rose hips, hibiscus, cinnamon, canella, and elderberry. The resulting tea will be like a robust, accented green tea with a tart finish.

Blend #5: A good green tea base can be accented with curcuma, goji berry, rose, strawberry, and cherry bits for a flavorful, fruity tea. Add in some turmeric if you want a slightly spicier version that isn't quite a black tea.

Black Tea Blends

Black tea blends tend to be bold and powerful, with spices, aggressive flavors, and fruit notes added to them to enhance their taste. Many of the chai blends you find are going to be a black tea, based on an Assam or Ceylon variety most likely.

Blend #1: Mix up some black tea with cinnamon, orange peel, and cloves. You'll get a delicious hot cinnamon spice tea with earthy notes and all of the health benefits of both tea and cinnamon. Orange helps to give you a secondary flavor profile, and the cloves give a hint of spice.

Blend #2: Take your basic black tea and mix it up with some peppermint or spearmint leaves, vanilla beans, and – if you're feeling bold around the holidays – a bit of candy cane ground up for a minty sugar infusion. Your new candy cane tea will be a holiday hit.

Blend #3: Take a black tea and mix in some dehydrated apple bits, some chopped almonds or almond powder, and a pinch of cinnamon. It might not seem like much at the outset, but if you're a fan of apple crisp for dessert, this tea will instantly remind you of that favored treat.

Blend #4: Mix up as many black teas as you can get your hands on. A blend of Ceylon, Assam, and Darjeeling, perhaps with even a hint of coffee bean, brings you what we like to call the English Breakfast tea. It's robust, heady, and a great way to wake up in the morning.

Blend #5: Maybe you want something a little less in-your-face with a black tea base. Start with a simple Assam and add in some ginger, lemongrass, and a hint of cardamom. This blend will bring to mind Thai cuisine, and pairs well when brewed in hot milk rather than water.

Herbal teas don't contain tea leaves, but the variety of different plants you can use in an herbal blend is almost limitless. Even plants you wouldn't typically think of as edible, like certain wildflowers, make great elements of herbal teas. They tend to have very delicate flavors, and are often smooth and fruity.

Blend #1: Mix up lavender, rose petals, and rose buds with a base of chamomile. This tea encourages peace, stress relief, and sleep, making it a great after dinner tea or a tea to sip on a stressful day.

Blend #2: Something similar to the above, you take a chamomile base and add rose buds, corn flowers, and orange peels. This is a light tea blend that brings citrus to mind and is almost like drinking a cup of orange juice with breakfast. It's an excellent beverage to accompany breakfast on a leisurely day where you don't need the caffeine to get up and moving.

Blend #3: Teas work great for everything from waking up to going to sleep, but what about teas meant to heal? An herbal blend of fennel, chamomile, and peppermint will be a pungent and healthy way to soothe a stomach ache or intestinal distress.

Blend #4: This blend is stacked with health benefits. Infuse your hot water with a mixture of turmeric and licorice root for a bold start, then add in some ginger for spice. Top it off with a balance of lemongrass and lemon and orange peels for a citrus candy flavor. Top the whole thing off with some honey when you brew it to sweeten it for best effect.

Exotic Mixtures

If you want something a little deeper in the tea world, or if you want to stack teas for additional effects and brew it strong, here are a couple of additional blends you can try:

Blend #1: This blend starts with a Sencha tea, a kind of leafy green tea favored in Japan. Mix it up with some oolong and some pu'erh, which will largely override the flavor. Why include the others? For the health benefits! To flavor this tea, add in peppermint, cinnamon, licorice root, and a combination of lemon myrtle, elderberry, hibiscus, and strawberry leaves. This result will still be missing a certain something, so add in apple, black currant, blackberry, raspberry, and orange oil. The total result is a pungent, aromatic tea with more notes than you can count, and it has a ton of health benefits.

Blend #2: Take some tea and ferment it for a while, and drink the resulting probiotic tea. Alright, so this one isn't really a blend you can make at home. Always be cautious with home fermentation; if you do it wrong, it can be dangerous to your health. Still, Kombucha – a kind of fermented tea beverage – has a variety of health benefits when you pick it up at a store.

The 7 Most Powerful Medicinal Tea Blends

Using a blend of herbs straight from your garden, you can treat a wide range of ailments by simply brewing a medicinal tea.

There are so many herbs that lay claim to aiding digestion or easing stomach aches. Many of the herbs listed below have been backed by science. Below are some common herbs that can be grown in the garden which can be used to treat a broad range of stomach problems, especially digestion and stomach aches.

- Ginger, lemon, and dandelion leaves are all bitter-tasting herbs, and it is this bitterness that stimulates bile and gastric acid production. This aids digestion by breaking down food. Ginger can also soothe and relax your intestines and has been found to prevent heartburn by tightening the esophagus muscle.

- Chamomile is easy to grow and can reduce stomach cramps, inflammation, and bloating. It is also known for its overall calming effect.

- Lemon balm has a slightly sweet, zesty taste, and has been used to treat digestion conditions for centuries. It has antioxidants and contains compounds that may reduce swelling and pain.

- Marshmallow root aids digestion by encouraging mucus production in the digestive tract. This soothes any irritated gut lining and inflammation.

- Eucalyptus leaves make a great tea which has the ability to ease and soothe the digestive tract. It contains antioxidants and has a fresh, minty taste.

- Peppermint and mint promote gases and bile to move through your body which eases bloating. They also work as antispasmodics to calm an upset stomach.

- Thyme is good for stomach aches and has been used to treat diarrhea throughout history. It tastes similar to rosemary, with a hint of mint or lemon.

Herbal Tea Blend for Digestion

- Place 1-2 slices of ginger, 1 sliced marshmallow root, and 2-3 dandelion leaves and flowers in a small pot of water and bring it to a boil.

- Add 2-3 chamomile flowers and lemon balm leaves, then simmer for 5 minutes.

- Remove from heat and add 1 sprig of thyme and 1-2 slices of lemon.

- Cover and allow to brew for 5 minutes.

- Add a small handful of either mint, peppermint, or eucalyptus leaves and brew for 3 –5 minutes.

- Strain and sweeten with honey if necessary.

Catnip, feverfew, and juniper berries can also be used to make an herbal tea for digestion.

2. Blood Pressure

The theophylline in black tea increases the flow of blood to the capillaries, and eucalyptus dilates your arteries. Both of them help lower blood pressure.

Hibiscus flowers have been proven to lower blood pressure and are also filled with antioxidants and anti-inflammatories.

Herbal Tea Blend for High Blood Pressure

- 1 regular black tea teabag.

- A small handful of hibiscus petals.

- A few fresh eucalyptus leaves.

- Place ingredients in a mug or small pot and pour boiling water over them.

- Allow to brew for 5 minutes.

- Strain and sweeten with honey.

3. Diabetes And Blood Sugar

Some people are able to manage their diabetes by going on a strict diet. Below are some common garden herbs that can help to regulate either insulin production or sugar absorption in your blood.

- Milk thistle can help people lower their blood sugar levels. It is packed with silymarin, which is an anti-inflammatory and an antioxidant. It has a very light, slightly bitter taste.
- Sage is light tasting and has been shown to lower blood sugar levels when taken over a long period.
- Cinnamon has been proven to improve your body's sensitivity to insulin and therefore can help diabetics to regulate its production. It is full of antioxidants. The sweet, nutty flavor goes well with milk thistle tea.
- Jasmine helps your body metabolize glucose, so it can prevent diabetes.

- Place a cinnamon stick in a pot of water and bring it to a boil very slowly (20 minutes).

- Remove from heat and brew for an additional 15 minutes. Remove the cinnamon stick when the water turns a dark, golden color.

- Bring the pot to a boil again, then remove from heat.

- Add a few milk thistle leaves, sage leaves, and fresh jasmine flowers and buds and brew for another 5 minutes.

- Strain and serve.

Another herbal tea blend that you can make to lower blood sugar levels includes hibiscus flowers, turmeric, ginger, lemongrass, stinging nettles, and eucalyptus leaves. These ingredients either hinder your body's ability to absorb sugar or regulate insulin production.

4. Cholesterol

High cholesterol is another health problem that can be managed with a strict diet. Its prevalence amongst the population means that a large amount of research has been performed on how some plants can lower cholesterol.

- Hibiscus tea is a common beverage for people with high cholesterol. It has a tart, refreshing taste that is similar to the taste of cranberries.
- Milk thistle has been studied for its ability to lower cholesterol.
- Both green tea and jasmine tea have both been found to lower cholesterol.
- Lemongrass helps to rid the body of toxins including cholesterol.
- Dandelion flowers and leaves can help your body to break down fats and cholesterol.

Herbal Tea Blend For Cholesterol

- Place a small handful of lemongrass and a few dandelion flowers and leaves into a pot of water and bring it to a boil.
- Simmer on a low heat for 5 minutes.
- Remove from heat and add a few milk thistle leaves, jasmine flowers, hibiscus petals, and a

regular green tea teabag. Cover and brew for 3 – 5 minutes.

- Strain and serve.

Other herbs and spices that can lower your cholesterol include Yerba Mate, cinnamon, and sage.

5. Respiratory Conditions Or Asthma

More and more people are discovering natural ways to minimize the symptoms of asthma and respiratory conditions. Drinking an herbal tea blend can soothe the throat and relax the airways.

- Licorice root makes saliva thicken and triggers mucus production which gently coats and soothes the airways. It also reduces inflammation. Licorice root can raise blood pressure if taken over a long period. Marshmallow root and honey can be used instead.

- The caffeine in black tea can provide up to 4 hours of relief. It works by relaxing the lungs and opening the airways.

- Ginger is an anti-inflammatory as well as an anti-histamine. It relaxes and soothes the throat and lungs.

- Eucalyptus and peppermint have antispasmodic properties that can relax muscles and open airways. They are both powerful decongestants by limiting the production of phlegm and breaking up mucus.

- Thyme reduces the duration of an asthma attack when taken over the long term.

Herbal Tea Blend For Asthma

- Place 1-2 slices of ginger and licorice root in a pot and bring to a boil.

- Add 1 sprig of thyme and simmer for 10 minutes.

- Remove from heat and add a regular black tea teabag and a small handful of either mint or eucalyptus leaves.

- Cover and allow to brew for 5 minutes.

- Strain and serve.

- Chamomile has long been used to reduce stomach cramps and aches thanks to its antispasmodic properties.
- Dandelion flowers and leaves can balance hormones to reduce menstrual cramps.
- Ginger helps to settle the stomach and menstrual cramps
- Yarrow flowers and sage have been used throughout history for menstrual cramps.
- Catnip, lavender, and raspberry leaves are all antispasmodic and relax the uterus.

Herbal Tea Blend For Menstrual Cramps

- Place 1-2 slices of ginger, 2-3 chamomile flowers, raspberry leaves, and dandelion flowers and leaves in a pot with water and bring to a boil.
- Simmer for 5 minutes.
- Remove from heat, add 2-3 yarrow and lavender flowers, cover, and brew for 5 minutes.
- Add a small handful of sage and catnip leaves and brew for 3 – 5 minutes.

- Strain and serve.

Red clover flowers can balance hormone levels to reduce menstrual cramps, however, they also act as a blood thinner, can make the birth control pill ineffective, and have also been linked to an increased risk of cancer of the uterus, so they shouldn't be consumed over long periods.

7. Headache

There are many different types of headaches that can be treated with certain herbal tea blends harvested from the garden.

- Ginger has been studied thoroughly, and it is as effective at reducing the pain from headaches as an over-the-counter medication.
- Studies show that feverfew can decrease the frequency and duration of a migraine. It has a bitter taste similar to chamomile.
- Lavender relaxes the body and can help with tension and stress headaches.
- Rosemary and sage can both help treat cluster headaches by increasing blood flow to the brain and decreasing inflammation.

- There is a link between the occurrence of headaches and migraines with low levels of magnesium. Alfalfa (Medicago sativa) is high in magnesium and has a very light, slightly bland taste.

- If taken at the onset of a headache, then taking a small amount of caffeine, like that found in a regular teabag, has been shown to reduce the severity of a headache.

Herbal Tea Blend for Headaches

- Place 1-2 slices of ginger, 2-3 feverfew flowers, and alfalfa leaves in a pot with water and bring to a boil.

- Simmer for 5 minutes.

- Remove from heat, add 2-3 lavender flowers, a sprig of rosemary and sage, and a regular teabag. Cover and brew for 5 minutes.

- Strain and serve.

White willow bark, butterbur, and ginkgo tea can also treat migraines and headaches.

We prepared 10 DIY recipes to make your own tea blend. You can use these recipes as guidelines and a starting point for blending. The amount of leaves used in recipes is enough for 2-3 infusions, depending on the recipe. Our recipes include the most common herbs, fruit and spices, for very easy blending. Every herb, fruit and spice is different, so it's important to adjust the amounts to best suit your taste. Intensity of ingredients will depend on the type, quality, storing conditions, etc. We suggest blending small amounts and trying them first.

1. Rose Breakfast Blend

Breakfast blends are usually a mix of stronger and lighter teas in the ratio that gives a recognizable breakfast tea flavor. The most common teas in breakfast blends come from India and Sri Lanka, although teas from other countries are now used as well. For the traditional Breakfast Blend, use Darjeeling and Assam tea. This tea is perfect with milk.

Ingredients:

- 2 teaspoons of Darjeeling tea (Namring Estate Darjeeling)
- 3 teaspoons of Assam tea (Organic Assam)
- ½ – 1 teaspoon of rose buds

Extra tip: Add guarana powder for an extra caffeine boost.

2. Tropical Pu'erh

If you want to drink pu'erh because of the benefits but don't quite enjoy the pure flavor, you can easily create your own blend with the flavor that you like the most. Our recommendation is coconut pu'erh because it blends well with the earthly flavor of ripe pu'erh. Adjust the ratio to suit your taste. You can exclude candied fruit and add coconut only.

Ingredients:

- 2 spoons of Pu'erh tea
- 1 teaspoon of candied pineapple
- 1 teaspoon of candied mango
- 1 teaspoon of shredded coconut

Fast blending: Blend pu'erh tea with your favorite fruit tea.

3. White Spice tea

Light flavor of white tea blends well with tangy and spicy notes. Peppercorns are a great choice for adding a spicy note and dried strawberries give a tangy and sweet layer to light and delicate flavor of Bai Mu Dan. This tea contains caffeine.

Ingredients:

- 2 spoons of Pai Mu Tan
- ½ teaspoon of peppercorns
- 1 teaspoon of dried strawberries
- A pinch of safflower

Extra tip: Do not use flavors and herbs with a strong taste for blending with white tea.

4. Apple Pie Herbal tea

Sunday dessert in a liquified form? Yes, please. Apple Pie herbal blend has rooibos as a base because of its natural sweet flavor. Besides, this dessert should be suitable for children as well, so we wanted to leave out teas with caffeine. It's easy to blend and makes a cup of tea with a delightful sweet and lightly tangy taste.

Ingredients:

- 2 spoons of Rooibos tea
- 1-2 teaspoon of dried apple
- 1 inch of cinnamon stick
- ½ inch of vanilla pod

Extra tip: Add white chocolate drops for a creamier and sweeter tea.

5. Minty Sencha

This minty blend is great both hot and cold, but for the ultimate summer refreshment use cold brewing technique to make an iced tea. For an extra kick add some dried spearmint leaves.

Ingredients:

- 1 teaspoon dried lemongrass
- 1 teaspoon of dried mint
- 2 spoons of Chinese Sencha Green

Extra tip: Add fresh cucumber to the jug or teapot when cold-brewing. Chinese sencha is better choice for blending than Japanese sencha.

6. Chamomile Herbal

If you are looking for a calming tea without a caffeine that you can drink in the evening, chamomile is the best herb to use. All the herbs in this blend offer calming and soothing properties, especially for the stomach problems. This blend is best hot.

Ingredients:

- 2 spoons of dried chamomile
- ½ teaspoon of dried licorice root
- 1 teaspoon of dried ginger root

Extra tip: For a more potent sleepy time tea replace ginger with valerian root.

7. Refreshing Hibiscus

Crimson color and refreshing tangy and fresh taste make this herbal blend one of the best summer drinks you can blend yourself. It's great both hot and cold.

Ingredients:

- 2 spoons dried hibiscus
- 1 teaspoon of mint leaves
- 1 teaspoon of lemongrass

Extra tip: This tea is great both hot and cold.

8. Upgraded Earl Grey

Earl Grey, the classical blend beloved by many tea drinkers, you can easily upgrade by adding a pinch of lavender flowers or rose petals. Be careful not to use too much flowers as they will ruin the taste. Both lavender and rose petals have a dominant scent and flavor and should be used in small amounts to add just an extra layer to your blend.

Ingredients:

- 2 teaspoons of regular Earl Grey tea (or feel free to use one of the nontraditional blends and enhance them with more ingredients)
- A pinch of Lavender or rose petals

Extra tip: Add safflower for an extra note.

The beauty of chai tea is that you can customize your recipe until you get the flavor you truly enjoy. Chai is always made with a black tea base, preferably with stronger Assam tea, milk and a blend of different spices. Crush the spices in a mortar and blend with black tea.

Ingredients:

- 3-5 spoons of Assam black tea
- 1 teaspoon of dried ginger
- ½ teaspoon of peppercorns
- 2 inches of cinnamon stick
- 1 teaspoon of cardamom
- 1 teaspoon of cloves

Extra tip: Add star anise, nutmeg, cocoa shells or vanilla to your blend. Adjust the ratio of spices to black tea leaves to create lighter or stronger taste.

Liquid chocolate in the healthiest way will satisfy your chocolate needs, especially during rainy cool days. Use boiling water to brew Herbal Chocolate tea to melt the chocolate drops.

Ingredients:

- 1 teaspoon of chocolate drops
- 2 spoons of pure Rooibos tea
- ½ – 1 inch of vanilla pod
- ½ teaspoons of cocoa shells

Extra tip: Turn this blend to an After Eight tea by adding a pinch of dried mint leaves. Replace rooibos with Yunnan Black tea if you want a stronger flavor and tea with caffeine. Make it in a latte style for extra creaminess.

The benefits of blending your own tea

With only 1-2 different pure teas and herbs, flowers and spices you can create numerous blends and enjoy different tea each day. Changing only one or two ingredients can change a tea from calming to invigorating. Blending is good for enhancing the flavor of tea you don't necessarily enjoy, but would like to drink because of the health benefits. You can find most of the ingredients for blending in health food stores or even grow your own herbs, collect flowers or dry fruit. This way you can reduce the risk of drinking tea with sweeteners or artificial flavors sometimes hidden in blends.

Lower Risk of Cancer

Green and black teas also contain important polyphenols, which are micronutrients that are found in plant-based foods. The polyphenols found in these types of tea have been associated with the healthy regulation of cancer cell growth and survival, leading to a lower risk of developing cancer.

Better Sleep Quality and Lower Risk of Depression

Some teas, including chamomile, are consumed to help people relax at the end of the day so they can sleep better and wind down. And chamomile tea has been found to help postpartum women get better sleep and alleviate their depression.

More Focus and Alertness

More research needs to be done to accurately understand the effects of caffeine on cognitive function. However, some studies have indicated that consuming caffeine found in some teas, in low doses and regularly, may contribute to better focus and alertness.

Potential Risks of Tea

Drinking tea doesn't have many health risks associated with it. However, because some teas have high levels of caffeine, including black tea and green tea, there are a few points to be aware of as you drink it.

Too Much Caffeine Intake

When you consume too much caffeine, you could experience symptoms like a faster heartbeat, tremors in your muscles, headache, nervousness, anxiety, and insomnia. However, these symptoms are more commonly associated with drinking a lot of coffee, which has substantially more caffeine than even the strongest teas.

Other than overconsuming caffeine, there are few risks associated with drinking tea. Enjoy a cup to hydrate your body and gain important minerals and microminerals.

Green Tea Shake

Recipe Summary

I am a big fan of Starbucks Green Tea Blended Creme Drinks, so I decided to create my own! Enjoy! :)

Prep:10 mins

Total:10 mins

Servings:2

Yield:2 servings

Ingredients

- 1 cup vanilla ice cream
- ¾ cup brewed green tea
- 3 tablespoons white sugar
- 2 drops green food coloring
- 12 cubes ice cubes

Directions

Step 1

Combine the ice cream, green tea, sugar, food coloring, and ice cubes in a blender. Blend on high until smooth.

Nutrition Facts

Per Serving: 206 calories; protein 2.3g; carbohydrates 34.6g; fat 7.3g; cholesterol 29mg; sodium 59.2mg.

Raghavan's Curry Blend

Recipe Summary

Try this easy blend in place of curry powder for brighter flavors.

Prep:5 mins

Total:5 mins

Servings:16

Yield:1 /4 cup

Ingredients

- 8 dried chile de arbol peppers, stemmed, crumbled
- 2 tablespoons coriander seeds
- 1 tablespoon cumin seeds
- 2 teaspoons yellow or black mustard seeds

- 1 teaspoon black peppercorns

- ½ teaspoon whole cloves

1 teaspoon ground turmeric

Directions

Step 1

Grind dried chiles de arbol, coriander seeds, cumin seeds, mustard seeds, peppercorns, and cloves in a spice grinder (or a coffee grinder or high-powered blender) to the consistency of finely ground black pepper. Stir in turmeric. Store in a sealed container in a cool, dark place up to 3 months.

Nutrition Facts

Per Serving: 57 calories; protein 2.3g; carbohydrates 8.9g; fat 0.4g; sodium 6.2mg.

Berbere Spice Blend
Recipe Summary

I love berbere spice, a classic Ethiopian spice blend, but it never occurred to me to make my own. Actually, traditional berbere spice would use whole spice seeds/pods that get toasted and ground. But I usually toast the spices during the cooking process. Berbere is one of the most delicious and versatile spice mixes ever.

Prep:10 mins

Total:10 mins

Servings:48

Yield:2 cups seasoning

Ingredients

- ½ cup ground dried New Mexico chiles
- ¼ cup paprika
- 1 tablespoon cayenne pepper
- 1 teaspoon onion powder
- 1 teaspoon ground ginger
- 1 teaspoon cumin
- 1 teaspoon ground coriander
- 1 teaspoon ground cardamom
- 1 teaspoon ground fenugreek
- ½ teaspoon garlic powder
- ½ teaspoon ground cinnamon

- ½ teaspoon ground allspice
- ½ teaspoon ground cloves
- ¼ teaspoon ground nutmeg

Directions

Step 1

Place ground chiles, paprika, and cayenne pepper into a bowl; stir. Add onion powder, ginger, cumin, coriander, cardamom, fenugreek, garlic powder, cinnamon, allspice, cloves, and nutmeg. Gently whisk together until thoroughly mixed.

Step 2

Store in an airtight container, preferably glass.

Chef's Note:

One of my favorite ways to use berbere spices is this Spiced Chicken Breasts recipe.

Nutrition Facts

Per Serving: 3 calories; protein 0.1g; carbohydrates 0.6g; fat 0.1g; sodium 0.5mg.

Recipe Summary

Prep: 10 mins

Cook: 25 mins

Additional: 15 mins

Total: 50 mins

Servings: 12

Yield: 12 muffins

Ingredients

- 1 ⅔ cups all-purpose flour
- ½ teaspoon salt
- 1 teaspoon baking powder
- 1 tablespoon matcha green tea powder, or to taste
- ½ cup white sugar
- 1 egg
- ⅓ cup melted butter
- 1 cup milk
- ¼ cup chopped walnuts (Optional)

Directions

Step 1

Preheat oven to 350 degrees F (175 degrees C). Grease 12 muffin cups, or line with paper muffin liners.

Step 2

Whisk the flour, salt, baking powder, matcha, and sugar together in a mixing bowl; set aside. Whisk together the egg, melted butter, and milk in another bowl. Stir the milk mixture into the flour mixture until just moistened. Stir in walnuts. Divide the batter among the prepared muffin cups.

Step 3

Bake in the preheated oven until golden and the tops spring back when lightly pressed, about 25 minutes. Cool in the muffin tin for 5 minutes, then remove to cool on a wire rack.

Nutrition Facts

Per Serving: 174 calories; protein 3.5g; carbohydrates 23.1g; fat 7.7g; cholesterol 30.7mg; sodium 188.6mg.

Recipe Summary

Prep: 45 mins

Cook: 20 mins

Additional: 2 hrs 15 mins

Total: 3 hrs 20 mins

Servings: 24

Yield: 2 pastries

Ingredients

For the Dough:

- 1 cup milk
- 1 egg, beaten
- 1 tablespoon butter, room temperature
- 3 tablespoons white sugar
- ½ teaspoon salt
- 3 ¼ cups bread flour
- ¾ teaspoon active dry yeast

For the Filling:

- 2 tablespoons butter, softened

- 2 teaspoons ground cinnamon

- ¾ cup packed brown sugar

- ½ cup raisins

For the Icing:

- 1 cup confectioners' sugar, sifted

- ½ teaspoon almond extract

- 1 tablespoon milk, or as needed

Directions

Step 1

In a bread machine, put milk, egg, butter, sugar, salt, bread flour, and yeast in the order suggested by the manufacturer. Select the Dough cycle and press Start. When dough is mixed, transfer to a greased bowl; cover with plastic wrap and let rise until doubled, about 1 to 1 1/2 hours.

Step 2

Grease 2 baking sheets or line them with parchment paper; set aside.

Step 3

Divide dough in half. Roll each piece out into rectangles about 12x16 inches. Spread each dough rectangle with 1 tablespoon softened butter. In a small bowl, combine 2 teaspoons ground cinnamon, 3/4 cup light brown sugar, and 1/2 cup raisins.

Step 4

Sprinkle cinnamon mixture onto buttered dough. Roll them up jelly-roll fashion, along long side. Pinch edges to seal. Stretch and twist into rings, pinching ends to seal. Place them seam-side down onto prepared baking sheets. Using clean scissors, cut 2/3 way of the way through the loaf at about 1-inch intervals. Spread each cut slightly. you wish to

Step 5

[At this point, the dough can be refrigerated: cover dough with greased plastic wrap and refrigerate overnight. The next morning, let pastries come to room temperature for about half an hour before baking as directed in step 7.]

Step 6

Alternately, cover each ring with a clean towel or greased plastic wrap and let loaves rise until double, about 40 minutes.

Step 7

Arrange two oven racks so that both baking sheets will fit. Preheat oven to 350 degrees F (175 degrees C).

Step 8

Bake for 10 minutes in preheated; rotate baking sheets. Bake until rings are light brown and the filling is oozing and bubbling, about 10 minutes more.

Step 9

In a small mixing bowl, combine confectioners sugar, almond extract, and milk until icing is desired consistency. Drizzle icing over warm pastries.

Cook's Note:

The first part of this recipe is prepared in my bread machine on Christmas Eve. I make it right up to the second rise stage, then cover and refrigerate it. On Christmas morning, I allow it to warm up and rise until double in size before baking. It is especially sumptuous when it is still warm and a special treat for Christmas morning in our house.

Editor's Note:

To prepare this recipe in a stand mixer, combine lukewarm milk and yeast in the mixing bowl; let stand five minutes. Add beaten egg, 1 tablespoon butter, 3 tablespoons white sugar, salt, and bread flour. With the dough hook, mix on low speed for 12 to 15 minutes, scraping down hook and sides of bowl occasionally. Transfer dough to a greased bowl to rise; proceed with recipe.

Nutrition Facts

Per Serving: 83 calories; protein 0.8g; carbohydrates 16.4g; fat 1.9g; cholesterol 12.4mg; sodium 68.4mg

Green-Tea Cupcakes

Recipe Summary

Prep: 25 mins

Cook: 20 mins

Additional: 1 hr 15 mins

Total: 2 hrs

Servings: 12

Yield: 12 cupcakes

Ingredients

- ¼ cup butter
- ¼ cup vegetable oil butter spread (such as Smart Balance®)
- ½ cup granular no-calorie sucralose sweetener (such as Splenda®)
- ½ cup white sugar
- 3 egg whites
- 1 teaspoon vanilla extract
- 1 teaspoon almond extract
- 1 ½ cups cake flour
- 2 teaspoons baking powder
- 2 tablespoons green tea powder (matcha)

* ½ cup nonfat milk

Directions

Step 1

Preheat an oven to 350 degrees F (175 degrees C). Grease 12 muffin cups, or line with paper muffin liners.

Step 2

Beat the butter, vegetable oil butter spread, sweetener, and sugar with an electric mixer in a large bowl until light and fluffy. The mixture should be noticeably lighter in color. Add the room-temperature egg whites one at a time, allowing each egg to blend into the butter mixture before adding the next. Beat in the vanilla and almond extracts with the last egg. Combine cake flour, baking powder, and green tea powder in a small bowl. Pour in the flour mixture alternately with the milk, mixing until just incorporated. Pour the batter into prepared pan.

Step 3

Bake in the preheated oven until a toothpick inserted into the center comes out clean, about 20 minutes. Cool in the pans for 10 minutes before removing to cool completely on a wire rack.

Nutrition Facts

Per Serving: 168 calories; protein 2.9g; carbohydrates 23.3g; fat 6.9g; cholesterol 10.7mg; sodium 174.2mg.

Iced Tea II

Recipe Summary

Prep: 10 mins

Cook: 1 hr

Total: 1 hr 10 mins

Servings: 8

Yield: 8 servings

Ingredients

- 8 cups water
- 3 orange pekoe tea bags
- ¾ cup white sugar
- ½ cup lemon juice

Directions

Step 1

In a large saucepan, heat water to a rapid boil. Remove from heat and drop in the tea bags. Cover and let steep for 1 hour.

Step 2

In a large pitcher, combine the steeped tea and the sugar. Stir until sugar is dissolved, then stir in lemon juice. Refrigerate until chilled.

Nutrition Facts

Per Serving: 76 calories; protein 0.1g; carbohydrates 20.1g; sodium 0.2mg.

Russian Tea Cakes

Recipe Summary

Prep: 20 mins

Cook: 15 mins

Additional: 15 mins

Total: 50 mins

Servings: 36

Yield: 3 dozen cookies

Ingredients

- 1 cup butter
- 1 teaspoon vanilla extract
- 2 cups all-purpose flour
- 6 tablespoons confectioners' sugar
- 1 cup chopped walnuts
- ⅓ cup confectioners' sugar for rolling

Directions

Step 1

Preheat the oven to 350 degrees F (175 degrees C).

Step 2

Cream butter and vanilla together in a medium bowl until smooth. Combine flour and the 6 tablespoons confectioners' sugar in another bowl; stir into the butter mixture until just blended. Mix in walnuts.

Step 3

Roll dough into 1-inch balls and place them 2 inches apart on ungreased cookie sheets.

Step 4

Bake for 12 minutes in the preheated oven. Cool cookies and roll in remaining confectioners' sugar. Roll cookies in confectioners' sugar a second time if desired.

Nutrition Facts

Per Serving: 102 calories; protein 1.3g; carbohydrates 8.2g; fat 7.3g; cholesterol 13.6mg; sodium 36.6mg.

Mississippi Tea Cakes

Recipe Summary

Prep: 15 mins

Cook: 10 mins

Additional: 25 mins

Total: 50 mins

Servings: 36

Yield: 3 dozen

Ingredients

- ½ cup butter, softened
- 1 cup white sugar
- 1 egg
- 1 teaspoon vanilla extract
- 2 cups all-purpose flour
- 1 teaspoon baking powder
- ½ teaspoon baking soda
- ¼ cup buttermilk

Directions

Step 1

Preheat oven to 350 degrees F (175 degrees C). Grease cookie sheets.

Step 2

In a medium bowl, cream together butter and sugar until smooth. Beat in egg and vanilla. Combine flour, baking powder, and baking soda; beat into the creamed mixture alternately with the buttermilk. Drop by rounded spoonfuls onto prepared cookie sheets.

Step 3

Bake for 8 to 10 minutes in preheated oven. Allow cookies to cool on baking sheets for 5 minutes before transferring to a wire rack to cool completely.

Nutrition Facts

Per Serving: 73 calories; protein 1g; carbohydrates 11g; fat 2.8g; cholesterol 12mg; sodium 53.1mg.

Smooth Sweet Tea

Recipe Summary

Prep: 5 mins

Additional: 3 hrs 15 mins

Total: 3 hrs 20 mins

Servings: 8

Yield: 8 cups

Ingredients

- 1 pinch baking soda
- 2 cups boiling water

- 6 tea bags

- ¾ cup white sugar

- 6 cups cool water

Directions

Step 1

Sprinkle a pinch of baking soda into a 64-ounce, heat-proof glass pitcher. Pour in boiling water and add tea bags. Cover and allow to steep for 15 minutes.

Step 2

Remove tea bags and discard; stir in sugar until dissolved. Pour in cool water; refrigerate until cold, about 3 hours.

Nutrition Facts

Per Serving: 73 calories; carbohydrates 18.7g; sodium 41.3mg.

Green Tea Cheesecake

Recipe Summary

Prep: 15 mins

Cook: 25 mins

Additional: 1 hr

Total: 1 hr 40 mins

Servings: 12

Yield: 1 - 9 inch cheesecake

Ingredients

- 2 (8 ounce) containers fat-free cream cheese, softened
- 2 eggs, beaten
- ¾ cup white sugar
- 1 tablespoon green tea powder
- 2 teaspoons vanilla extract
- 1 (9 inch) prepared graham cracker pie crust

Directions

Step 1

Preheat oven to 350 degrees F (175 degrees C).

Step 2

In a large bowl, beat together the cream cheese and sugar until smooth. Mix in the green tea powder, eggs, and vanilla extract until lightly and creamy; pour into the prepared crust.

Step 3

Bake in preheated oven for 25 minutes, or until the center jiggles evenly when the cake is shaken lightly. Refrigerate 1 hour before serving.

Nutrition Facts

Per Serving: 197 calories; protein 7.3g; carbohydrates 27.9g; fat 6.3g; cholesterol 34mg; sodium 329.1mg

Mississippi Tea Cakes

Recipe Summary

Prep: 15 mins

Cook: 10 mins

Additional: 25 mins

Total: 50 mins

Servings: 36

Yield: 3 dozen

Ingredients

- ½ cup butter, softened
- 1 cup white sugar
- 1 egg
- 1 teaspoon vanilla extract
- 2 cups all-purpose flour
- 1 teaspoon baking powder
- ½ teaspoon baking soda
- ¼ cup buttermilk

Directions

Step 1

Preheat oven to 350 degrees F (175 degrees C). Grease cookie sheets.

Step 2

In a medium bowl, cream together butter and sugar until smooth. Beat in egg and vanilla. Combine flour, baking powder, and baking soda; beat into the creamed mixture alternately with the buttermilk. Drop by rounded spoonfuls onto prepared cookie sheets.

Step 3

Bake for 8 to 10 minutes in preheated oven. Allow cookies to cool on baking sheets for 5 minutes before transferring to a wire rack to cool completely.

Nutrition Facts

Per Serving: 73 calories; protein 1g; carbohydrates 11g; fat 2.8g; cholesterol 12mg; sodium 53.1mg.

Hawaiian Iced Tea

Recipe Summary

Prep: 10 mins

Additional: 1 hr 35 mins

Total: 1 hr 45 mins

Servings: 8

Yield: 8 servings

Ingredients

- 1 quart barely boiling hot water
- 4 orange pekoe tea bags

- 1 quart ice cold water

- 1 (16 ounce) can pineapple juice

- ½ cup simple syrup

- 1 fresh pineapple - peeled, cored, and cut into spears

Direction

Step 1

Pour the barely boiling hot water into a large pitcher, and add the tea bags. Steep the tea, 2 to 4 minutes. Remove the tea bags and pour in the ice water. Pour in the pineapple juice. Refrigerate until thoroughly chilled, about 1 1/2 hours.

Step 2

Pour the tea over ice, garnish with pineapple spears, and serve.

Cook's Note:

It's easy to make your own versatile sweetener for ice tea and other drinks with this recipe for Simple Syrup.

Nutrition Facts

Per Serving: 152 calories; protein 1.1g; carbohydrates 39.3g; fat 0.3g; sodium 10.4mg.

Recipe Summary

Prep: 1 min

Cook: 1 min

Total: 2 mins

Servings: 2

Yield: 2 cups

Ingredients

- 1 cup soy milk
- 1 cup water
- 1 tablespoon green tea powder (matcha)
- 2 tablespoons white sugar

Directions

Step 1

In a small saucepan, combine the soy milk, water, green tea powder and sugar. Warm over medium heat while whisking until hot and foamy. Pour into mugs and enjoy.

Nutrition Facts

Per Serving: 119 calories; protein 4.4g; carbohydrates 20.8g; fat 2.2g; sodium 66.4mg

Smooth Sweet Tea

Recipe Summary

Prep: 5 mins

Additional: 3 hrs 15 mins

Total: 3 hrs 20 mins

Servings: 8

Yield: 8 cups

Ingredients

- 1 pinch baking soda
- 2 cups boiling water
- 6 tea bags
- ¾ cup white sugar

- 6 cups cool water

Directions

Step 1

Sprinkle a pinch of baking soda into a 64-ounce, heat-proof glass pitcher. Pour in boiling water and add tea bags. Cover and allow to steep for 15 minutes.

Step 2

Remove tea bags and discard; stir in sugar until dissolved. Pour in cool water; refrigerate until cold, about 3 hours.

Nutrition Facts

Per Serving: 73 calories; carbohydrates 18.7g; sodium 41.3mg.

Black Tea Lemonade

Recipe Summary

Prep: 5 mins

Cook: 5 mins

Additional: 2 hrs

Total: 2 hrs 10 mins

Servings: 8

Yield: 8 servings

Ingredients

- 5 cups water
- ½ cup white sugar
- 3 orange pekoe tea bags
- 1 (12 ounce) can frozen lemonade concentrate
- 5 cups water

Directions

Step 1

Bring 5 cups of water and the sugar to a boil in a saucepan, then remove from the heat and add the tea bags. Allow tea to steep while you mix the lemonade concentrate and remaining water in a large pitcher. Pour the tea mixture into the lemonade, discarding tea bags. Stir and refrigerate until cold before serving.

Nutrition Facts

Per Serving: 148 calories; protein 0.2g; carbohydrates 38.2g; fat 0.1g; sodium 11.1mg.

Greek Seasoning Blend

Recipe Summary

Prep: 5 mins

Total: 5 mins

Servings:8

Yield: 1/3 cup

Ingredients

- 2 teaspoons salt
- 2 teaspoons garlic powder
- 2 teaspoons dried basil
- 2 teaspoons dried Greek oregano
- 1 teaspoon ground cinnamon
- 1 teaspoon ground black pepper
- 1 teaspoon dried parsley
- 1 teaspoon dried rosemary, minced
- 1 teaspoon dried dill weed
- 1 teaspoon dried marjoram

- 1 teaspoon cornstarch
- ½ teaspoon ground thyme
- ½ teaspoon ground nutmeg

Directions

Step 1

Place salt, garlic powder, basil, oregano, cinnamon, black pepper, parsley, rosemary, dill, marjoram, cornstarch, thyme, and nutmeg in a small bowl; mix well.

Step 2

Transfer to an airtight container for storage.

Nutrition Facts

Per Serving: 9 calories; protein 0.3g; carbohydrates 1.9g; fat 0.2g; sodium 582.6mg.

Blended Strawberry Daiquiri

Recipe Summary

Prep: 5 mins

Total: 5 mins

Servings: 1

Yield: 1 serving

Ingredients

- 1 cup ice
- 5 strawberries
- 2 fluid ounces white rum
- 1 fluid ounce lime juice
- ½ fluid ounce triple sec
- ½ teaspoon confectioners' sugar

Directions

Step 1

Blend ice, strawberries, rum, lime juice, triple sec, and confectioners' sugar in a blender at high speed until smooth, about 30 seconds.

Nutrition Facts

Per Serving: 223 calories; protein 0.7g; carbohydrates 17.4g; fat 0.3g; sodium 10.5mg.

Blended Berry Pancakes

Recipe Summary

Prep: 10 mins

Cook: 30 mins

Total: 40 mins

Servings: 4

Yield: 8 pancakes

Ingredients

- 1 cup pancake mix
- ¾ cup water
- 10 whole frozen strawberries
- ½ cup frozen blueberries
- 1 teaspoon brown sugar, or to taste (Optional)

Directions

Step 1

Preheat a pancake griddle to medium heat. Whisk together the pancake mix and water in a bowl.

Step 2

Place the still-frozen strawberries into a blender, and pulse several times to break the berries up into small pieces. Mix the chopped strawberries and the frozen blueberries into the batter until the fruit is well distributed.

Step 3

Grease the griddle with butter, and pour about 1/4 cup of batter per pancake onto the griddle. Allow the bottom side to brown and the batter to form air holes; sprinkle the uncooked side with brown sugar, if desired, and flip to brown the other side.

Cook's Note

Brown sugar can also be tossed with banana slices,and cooked on a greased medium-heat pan to create warm, candied banana slices to top the berry pancakes.

Nutrition Facts

Per Serving: 144 calories; protein 3.1g; carbohydrates 31.5g; fat 0.8g; sodium 486mg.

Chicken Seasoning Blend

Recipe Summary

Prep: 5 mins

Total: 5 mins

Servings: 6

Yield: 2 tablespoons

Ingredients

- 1 ½ teaspoons sea salt
- 1 teaspoon dried basil
- 1 teaspoon crushed dried rosemary
- ½ teaspoon garlic powder
- ½ teaspoon dry mustard powder
- ½ teaspoon paprika
- ½ teaspoon ground black pepper
- ½ teaspoon ground dried thyme
- ¼ teaspoon celery seed
- ¼ teaspoon dried parsley
- ⅛ teaspoon ground cumin
- ⅛ teaspoon cayenne pepper
- ⅛ teaspoon chicken bouillon granules

Directions

Step 1

Mix salt, basil, rosemary, garlic powder, mustard powder, paprika, black pepper, thyme, celery seed, parsley, cumin, cayenne pepper, and chicken bouillon together in a small bowl until blended.

Nutrition Facts

Per Serving: 6 calories; protein 0.3g; carbohydrates 0.8g; fat 0.2g; sodium 448.5mg.

Berbere Spice Blend

Recipe Summary

Prep: 32 mins

Total: 32 mins

Servings: 48

Yield: 2 cups seasoning

Ingredients

- ½ cup ground dried New Mexico chiles
- ¼ cup paprika
- 1 tablespoon cayenne pepper
- 1 teaspoon onion powder

- 1 teaspoon ground ginger
- 1 teaspoon cumin
- 1 teaspoon ground coriander
- 1 teaspoon ground cardamom
- 1 teaspoon ground fenugreek
- ½ teaspoon garlic powder
- ½ teaspoon ground cinnamon
- ¼ teaspoon ground nutmeg
- ½ teaspoon ground allspice
- ½ teaspoon ground cloves

Directions

Step 1

Place the ground chilies, paprika, and cayenne pepper into a bowl; stir. Add onion powder, ginger, cumin, coriander, cardamom, fenugreek, garlic powder, cinnamon, nutmeg, allspice, and cloves. Gently whisk together until thoroughly mixed.

Step 2

Store in an airtight container, preferably glass.

Chef's Note:

One of my favorite ways to use berbere spices is this Spiced Chicken Breasts recipe.

Nutrition Facts

Per Serving: 3 calories; protein 0.1g; carbohydrates 0.6g; fat 0.1g; sodium 0.5mg

Raghavan's Curry Blend

Recipe Summary

Prep: 5 mins

Total: 5 mins

Servings: 16

Yield: 1 /4 cup

Ingredients

- 8 dried chile de arbol peppers, stemmed, crumbled
- 2 tablespoons coriander seeds
- 1 tablespoon cumin seeds
- 2 teaspoons yellow or black mustard seeds
- 1 teaspoon black peppercorns

- ½ teaspoon whole cloves
- 1 teaspoon ground turmeric

Directions

Step 1

Grind dried chiles de arbol, coriander seeds, cumin seeds, mustard seeds, peppercorns, and cloves in a spice grinder (or a coffee grinder or high-powered blender) to the consistency of finely ground black pepper. Stir in turmeric. Store in a sealed container in a cool, dark place up to 3 months.

Nutrition Facts

Per Serving: 57 calories; protein 2.3g; carbohydrates 8.9g; fat 0.4g; sodium 6.2mg

Creole Seasoning Blend

Recipe Summary

Prep: 5 mins

Total: 5 mins

Servings: 20

Yield: 1 1/4 cups

Ingredients

- 5 tablespoons paprika
- 3 tablespoons salt
- 2 tablespoons onion powder
- 2 tablespoons garlic powder
- 2 tablespoons dried oregano
- 2 tablespoons dried basil
- 1 tablespoon dried thyme
- 1 tablespoon black pepper
- 1 tablespoon white pepper
- 1 tablespoon cayenne pepper

Directions

Step 1

Combine paprika, salt, onion powder, garlic powder, oregano, basil, thyme, black pepper, white pepper, and cayenne pepper.

Step 2

Store in an airtight container.

Nutrition Facts

Per Serving: 16 calories; protein 0.7g; carbohydrates 3.4g; fat 0.4g; sodium 1048.2mg

Mango Craze Juice Blend

Recipe Summary

Prep: 5 mins

Total: 5 mins

Servings: 4

Yield: 5 cups

Ingredients

- 3 cups diced mango
- 1 ½ cups chopped fresh or frozen peaches
- ¼ cup chopped orange segments
- ¼ cup chopped and pitted nectarine
- ½ cup orange juice
- 2 cups ice

Directions

 Step 1

Place mango, peaches, orange, nectarine, orange juice, and ice into a blender. Blend for 1 minute, or until smooth.

Nutrition Facts

Per Serving: 150 calories; protein 1.3g; carbohydrates 38.4g; fat 0.6g; sodium 5.7mg.

Mango Craze Juice Blend

Recipe Summary

Prep: 5 mins

Total: 5 mins

Servings: 4

Yield: 5 cups

Ingredients

- 3 cups diced mango
- 1 ½ cups chopped fresh or frozen peaches
- ¼ cup chopped orange segments
- ¼ cup chopped and pitted nectarine
- ½ cup orange juice
- 2 cups ice

Directions

 Step 1

Place mango, peaches, orange, nectarine, orange juice, and ice into a blender. Blend for 1 minute, or until smooth.

Nutrition Facts

Per Serving: 150 calories; protein 1.3g; carbohydrates 38.4g; fat 0.6g; sodium 5.7mg.

Kate's Kickin' Spice Blend

Recipe Summary

Prep: 5 mins

Total: 5 mins

Servings: 14

Yield: 14 tablespoons

Ingredients

- 2 ½ tablespoons chili powder
- 2 tablespoons ground black pepper
- 2 tablespoons dried oregano

- 1 ½ tablespoons ground cumin
- 1 ½ tablespoons salt
- 1 ½ tablespoons garlic powder
- 1 ½ tablespoons onion powder
- 1 ½ tablespoons cayenne pepper

Directions

Step 1

Mix chili powder, black pepper, oregano, cumin, salt, garlic powder, onion powder, and cayenne pepper together in an airtight container.

Nutrition Facts

Per Serving: 18 calories; protein 0.7g; carbohydrates 3.6g; fat 0.6g; sodium 764.2mg.

Peach Tea

Recipe Summary

Prep: 5 mins

Cook: 15 mins

Total: 20 mins

Servings: 10

Yield: 1 gallon

Ingredients

- 3 cups wate
- 3 family size tea bags
- 2 fresh peaches - peeled, pitted, and sliced
- 1 cup water
- 1 ½ teaspoons stevia powder

Directions

Step 1

Bring 3 cups water to a boil in a saucepan over high heat. Add the tea bags, and steep for 15 minutes. Remove tea bags.

Step 2

Meanwhile, place peaches with 1 cup water into the jar of a blender, and blend until very smooth. Pour the peach mixture, tea, and stevia powder into a 1 gallon pitcher. Fill the pitcher to the top with water, and stir until blended.

Nutrition Facts

Per Serving: 5 calories; carbohydrates 1.6g; sodium 0.8mg.

Tea Cakes

Recipe Summary

Prep: 10 mins

Cook: 5 mins

Total: 15 mins

Servings: 24

Yield: 2 dozen tea cakes

Ingredients

- 1 cup butter, softened
- 1 ½ cups white sugar
- 3 cups all-purpose flour
- 1 teaspoon vanilla extract
- 1 teaspoon baking powder
- ½ teaspoon baking soda

Directions

Step 1

Preheat oven to 350 degrees F (175 degrees C). Grease a baking sheet.

Step 2

Beat butter and sugar in a bowl until creamy. Stir in flour, vanilla extract, baking powder, and baking soda until dough is well mixed. Drop spoonfuls of dough 2 inches apart onto prepared baking sheet.

Step 3

Bake in preheated oven until lightly browned, 5 to 10 minutes.

Nutrition Facts

Per Serving: 174 calories; protein 1.7g; carbohydrates 24.5g; fat 7.8g; cholesterol 20.3mg; sodium 101.3mg.

Tea Punch

Recipe Summary

Prep: 30 mins

Additional: 4 hrs

Total: 4 hrs 30 mins

Servings: 24

Yield: 24 servings

Ingredients

- 1 cup white sugar
- 1 cup strong brewed black tea
- 4 cups orange juice
- 4 cups pineapple juice
- 4 cups prepared lemonade
- 1 (2 liter) bottle ginger ale, chilled

Directions

Step 1

In a pitcher, combine sugar and tea. Stir until sugar is dissolved. Stir in orange juice, pineapple juice and lemonade. Chill in refrigerator for 4 hours.n

Step 2

Just before serving, pour chilled juice mixture into a punch bowl and stir in ginger ale.n

Nutrition Facts

Per Serving: 118 calories; protein 0.5g; carbohydrates 29.4g; fat 0.1g; sodium 13.1mg

Tea Biscuits

Recipe Summary

Servings: 20

Yield: 20 biscuits

Ingredients

- 2 cups all-purpose flou
- 4 teaspoons baking powder
- 1 teaspoon salt
- ½ cup shortening
- ¾ cup milk

Directions

Step 1

Preheat oven to 400 degrees F (205 degrees C). Grease a baking sheet.

Step 2

Combine flour, baking powder, and salt. Cut shortening in until mixture has a fine crumb texture. Stir in milk with a fork to make a soft dough. Knead 8 to 10 times, and then roll out to a thickness of at least 1/2 inch. Cut into rounds with a cookie or biscuit cutter. Place on cookie sheet, and allow to rest for a few minutes.

Step 3

Bake for 12 to 15 minutes. Serve warm.

Nutrition Facts

Per Serving: 96 calories; protein 1.6g; carbohydrates 10.2g; fat 5.4g; cholesterol 0.7mg; sodium 217.8mg.

Whisky Tea

Recipe Summary

Cook: 2 mins

Total: 2 mins

Servings: 1

Yield: 1 serving

Ingredients

- 1 cup boiling water

- 1 tea bag

- 1 (1.5 fluid ounce) jigger Irish whiskey

- 1 tablespoon milk

- 1 teaspoon white sugar

Directions

Step 1

Pour boiling water into a mug, and place the tea bag in to steep for about 1 minute. Remove and discard the tea bag. Pour in the whiskey, milk and sugar as desired. Stir, drink, give me good rating, then relax.

Nutrition Facts

Per Serving: 129 calories; protein 0.5g; carbohydrates 4.9g; fat 0.3g; cholesterol 1.2mg; sodium 13.4mg.

Salt-Free Spicy Herb Seasoning Blend

Recipe Summary

Prep: 10 mins

Total: 10 mins

Servings: 64

Yield: 64 servings

Ingredients

- 4 teaspoons sesame seeds
- 2 teaspoons celery seed
- 2 teaspoons Italian seasonin
- 2 teaspoons dried parsley flakes
- 1 teaspoon poppy seeds
- 1 teaspoon ground black pepper
- 1 teaspoon onion powder
- 1 teaspoon red pepper flakes
- ¾ teaspoon granulated garlic powder
- ¾ teaspoon paprika

Directions

Step 1

Mix sesame seeds, celery seed, Italian seasoning, dried parsley, poppy seeds, ground black pepper, onion powder, red pepper flakes, garlic powder, and paprika together in a bowl until well combined. Store in an airtight container for up to 6 months.

Nutrition Facts

Per Serving: 2 calories; protein 0.1g; carbohydrates 0.2g; fat 0.1g; sodium 0.3mg.

Russian Tea (No Mixes)

Recipe Summary

Prep: 5 mins

Cook: 10 mins

Additional: 20 mins

Total: 35 mins

Servings: 16

Yield: 1 gallon

Ingredients

- 1 gallon water, divided
- 4 family-size tea bags
- 2 cups white sugar

- 1 cinnamon stick
- 1 teaspoon whole cloves
- 2 cups pineapple juice
- 2 cups orange juice
- ¼ cup lemon juice

Directions

Step 1

Boil 2 quarts water in a pot. Remove from heat, add tea bags, and steep for 20 minutes. Remove and discard tea bags.n

Step 2

Combine remaining 2 quarts water, sugar, cinnamon stick, and cloves in a separate pot. Bring to a boil. Add the brewed tea, pineapple juice, orange juice, and lemon juice.n

Nutrition Facts

Per Serving: 129 calories; protein 0.4g; carbohydrates 32.8g; fat 0.1g; sodium 8.4mg

Recipe Summary

Prep: 5 mins

Cook: 10 mins

Additional: 5 mins

Total: 20 mins

Servings: 1

Yield: 1 serving

Ingredients

- 8 ounces apple cider
- 1 (2 inch) piece fresh ginger, peeled and sliced
- 1 (2 g) bag green tea

Directions

 Step 1

Combine apple cider and ginger in a saucepan; bring to a boil. Boil for 1 to 2 minutes.

Step 2

Place tea bag in a mug. Pour boiling cider into the mug, straining out the ginger slices. Steep for 1 to 2 minutes. Remove tea bag.

Cook's Note:

You can use 1/2 apple cider and half water, if desired to modify sweetness.

Nutrition Facts

Per Serving: 133 calories; protein 0.2g; carbohydrates 33.1g; fat 0.1g; sodium 27.4mg.

Black Tea Lemonade

Recipe Summary

Prep: 5 mins

Cook: 5 mins

Additional: 2 hrs

Total: 2 hrs 10 mins

Servings: 8

Yield: 8 servings

Ingredients

- 5 cups water
- ½ cup white sugar
- 3 orange pekoe tea bags
- 1 (12 ounce) can frozen lemonade concentrate
- 5 cups water

Directions

Step 1

Bring 5 cups of water and the sugar to a boil in a saucepan, then remove from the heat and add the tea bags. Allow tea to steep while you mix the lemonade concentrate and remaining water in a large pitcher. Pour the tea mixture into the lemonade, discarding tea bags. Stir and refrigerate until cold before serving.

Nutrition Facts

Per Serving: 148 calories; protein 0.2g; carbohydrates 38.2g; fat 0.1g; sodium 11.1mg.

Tea Leaf Eggs

Recipe Summary

Prep: 10 mins

Cook: 2 hrs 45 mins

Total: 2 hrs 55 mins

Servings: 10

Yield: 10 eggs

Ingredients

- 1 tablespoon black tea leaves
- 2 (3 inch) cinnamon sticks
- 4 whole star anise pods
- 1 tablespoon five-spice powder
- 6 whole cloves
- 1 slice fresh ginger root
- ½ teaspoon Szechuan peppercorns
- 1 teaspoon licorice root
- 1 piece dried mandarin orange peel
- 1 ounce Chinese rock sugar
- ½ cup dark soy sauce
- ⅓ cup light-colored soy sauce
- 10 hard-cooked eggs

Directions

Step 1

Place the tea, cinnamon, star anise, five-spice, cloves, ginger, peppercorns, licorice, orange peel, rock sugar, dark soy sauce, and light soy sauce in a large saucepan. Bring to a boil, then reduce heat to medium-low, and let simmer for 15 minutes. Meanwhile, lightly tap the hard-cooked eggs to crack the shells all over. The soy sauce will penetrate the cracks, and color the egg white.

Step 2

Place the eggs in the simmering liquid, and cook for 30 minutes, then remove from the heat, and let the eggs stand in the liquid for 2 hours off the heat. After 2 hours, drain the eggs, chill, and peel.

Nutrition Facts

Per Serving: 98 calories; protein 6.6g; carbohydrates 5.6g; fat 5.5g; cholesterol 212mg; sodium 1260.7mg.

Tea provides more than just a relaxing pause in our daily routines. With every cup, we're also giving our bodies a boost – and not just from caffeine. Tea blending is an essential aspect and part of the tea industry. It is what makes tea commercial and appealing to a larger number of consumers. The main three reasons tea blending occurs and important are: to ensure consistency in the quality of a tea batch on a grand scale; to introduce the health aspect to the art of drinking and blending tea; and a way to commercialize tea.

The whole idea surrounding tea blending is to create a distinct flavor and aroma, a perfect combination of tea, herbs, and spices that will a distinct and unique flavor profile and character. Whether store-bought or homemade, tea blends offer exceptional tea-drinking experience and a festival for all of your senses.

If you decide to blend tea at home, remember to have fun and stay open-minded to all sorts of new flavors and aromas you will surely discover in the process. Tea blending is art, a rule-free game and it very important to be fearless and just go for it. Not to mention that these blends are not only good for hot brews, but also for cold ones. So, use your favorite blend brew for a cozy night in, or as a refreshing conversation-starter for your friends.